Afghanistan-Taliban:

The War Within

By Lynn R. Hernandez

All rights reserved. No part of this publication may be reproduced, distributed or transmitted in any form or by any means, including photocopying, recording or other electronic or mechanical methods, without the prior written permission of the publisher, except in the case of brief quotations embodied in critical reviews and certain other non-commercial uses permitted by copyright law.

This book is dedicated to the beautiful souls whose lives were cut short as a result of this war. May their souls rest in perfect peace.

Chapter 10: Afghanistan Economy on the Brink of Collapse

"War must be, while we defend our lives against a destroyer who would devour all; but I do not love the bright sword for its sharpness, nor the arrow for its swiftness, nor the warrior for his glory. I love only that which they defend."

-J.R.R. Tolkien.

Part 1: A False Taste of Victory

Chapter I: "Who are the Taliban"?

The Taliban is a Sunni Islamist nationalist and pro-Pashtun organization created in the early 1990s that governed much of Afghanistan from 1996 to October 2001. The movement's basic nucleus—the name "Taliban" from Pashto for "students"was made of peasant farmers and men studying Islam at Afghan and Pakistani madrasas, or religious institutions. The Taliban developed a foothold and strengthened its dominance in southern Afghanistan. Ṭālebān ("Students"), sometimes written Taliban, an ultraconservative political and religious party that developed in Afghanistan in the mid-1990s after the departure of Soviet forces, the fall of Afghanistan's communist state, and the consequent breakdown in civil order. It originated as a tiny army of Afghan religious students and academics trying to challenge crime and corruption; the faction owes its name, Taliban (Pashto: Ṭālebān, "Students"), to its founding members.

Founders of Taliban

Mullah Omar

Biographical data concerning Mullah Omar is scant and inconsistent. He was an ethnic Pashtun of the Ghilzay branch who was born near Kandahār, in about 1950. Afghanistan. He is considered to have received limited schooling, except for his religious education in a madrasah (school of Islamic studies), which was halted by the Soviet invasion of Afghanistan in 1979.

Mullah Muhammad Omar Mujahid was an Afghan cleric, Islamist partisan combatant, and political leader. He formed the Islamic Emirate of Afghanistan (Taliban) and served as its first leader until his death.

After the Soviet pullout, Mullah Omar taught at a tiny hamlet madrasah in the district of Kandahār. The end of the war did not bring calm, however, and political and ethnic violence escalated thereafter. Claiming to have had a vision instructing him to restore peace, Mullah Omar led a group of madrasah students in the takeover of cities throughout the mid-1990s, including Kandahār, Herāt, Kabul, and Mazār-e Sharīf. In 1996 a shūrā (council) acknowledged Mullah Omar as amīr al-muʾminīn ("commander of the faithful"), a very symbolic title in the Muslim world that had been in usage since the collapse of the caliphate in 1924. That title also gave him emir of Afghanistan, which from October 1997 until the collapse of the Taliban was known as the Islamic Emirate of Afghanistan. Mullah Omar honored the event by taking what was considered to be the cloak of the Prophet Muhammad from the mosque in Kandahār where it was preserved and wearing the relic, thereby signifying himself as Muhammad's successor.

In the 1980s, Omar joined the Afghan mujahideen in their struggle against the Soviet Union and the Democratic Republic of Afghanistan. He lost his right eye in an explosion during the Soviet-Afghan War, and by 1995 had seized most of southern and western Afghanistan. After the Taliban took the Afghan capital Kabul in September 1996, Omar was declared the leader of the state of Afghanistan. During his stint as Afghanistan's ruler, Omar hardly left the city of Kandahar, where he stayed in a huge home reputedly provided for him by Osama bin Laden, the Saudi fighter who was the founder of al-Qaeda

Under Mullah Omar's leadership, Pashtun social standards (Pashtunwali) were essential, and stringent Islamic rules were enforced. Education and work for women all but disappeared; the death penalty was legislated for offenses like adultery and conversion away from Islam; and music, television, and other kinds of popular amusement were forbidden. Among his most controversial choices was an order to remove the huge Buddha sculptures at Bamiyan, culturally valuable artifacts of Afghanistan's pre-Islamic past. To the vocal sadness of the world community, they were destroyed in March 2001.

The quick conquest of Afghanistan by the Taliban under Mullah Omar is thought to have been supported at least in part by Bin Laden, who had transferred his headquarters to Afghanistan following his expulsion from Sudan in the mid-1990s. In the wake of al-Qaeda's September 11 attacks on New York City and Washington, D.C., Mullah Omar's refusal to extradite bin Laden prompted the United States to launch a series of military operations in Afghanistan. The Taliban government was overthrown, and Mullah Omar fled, he delegated all the operational control of the Taliban to his deputies, including Obaidullah Akhund. Omar fled from Kandahar to Zabulhi Province and his wives moved to Pakistan, but the Taliban continued to claim him as their leader, despite him taking almost no active role in the movement. Although the US put a $ 10 million bounty on Omar's head, he hid within walking distance of US bases in Zabul Province. He lived as a virtual hermit there, refusing visits from his family. On rare occasions, he would communicate with the Taliban leadership based in Quetta, Pakistan. During the first four years of the Taliban insurgency, he lived in a secret room of a home in Qalat, Zabul. When the US Armed Forces began building Forward Operating Base Lagman just a few hundred meters from his hideout, he decided to move. He relocated to a shack in a riverside hamlet in Shinkay District, southeast of Qalat. Soon after, US forces started building another base, FOB Wolverine, just 3 miles (5 km) away from him, but he did not move this time. To avoid detection, he would occasionally hide in the underground irrigation channels connected to his new shelter. Omar died of illness in April 2013 and was buried in a featureless grave. His death, however, remained concealed until July 2015, during which time the Taliban continued to issue statements in his name. Known for his reclusivity, he was (and remains) a mythical and revered figure within the Taliban.

Abdul Ghani Baradar

Abdul Ghani Baradar also called Mullah Baradar Akhund, born 29 September 1963 or c. 1968 is an Afghan political and religious leader who was the acting first deputy prime minister with Abdul Salam Hanafi and Abdul Kabir, of Afghanistan. He is also a co-founder of the Taliban. He is known by the honorific Mullah. He was Mullah Omar's senior deputy from 2002 to 2010, and since 2019 he has been the Taliban's fourth-in-command, as the third of Leader Hibatullah Akhundzada's three deputies.

Baradar's Early engagement in the Taliban

Baradar started his military career as a guerrilla fighter in the Afghan War (1978–92) when he fought in a unit of the mujahideen that also featured Mohammad Omar and others who would later become founding members of the Taliban. As the battle quiet down, members of the unit found opportunities in Islamic instruction (madrasah) in the Maywand area (near the city of Kandahār). But postwar Afghanistan was far from tranquil as the new Afghan government fought to exert power outside of Kabul. Extortion, abduction, and assault all became widespread as militias and warlords overran most of the nation. Along with scores of others participating in the local madrasahs, Omar, Baradar, and other members of their old unit took up guns against a local warlord in 1994 and started to pacify the region. As the band collected support and moved beyond Maywand, it became known as the Taliban (Pashto: Ṭālebān ["Students"]) because of its affiliation with madrasah students. From the outset of the movement, Baradar was one of its most recognized and accomplished guerilla leaders.

Quickly seizing control over much of Afghanistan, the Taliban took Kabul in 1996 and ousted the government. The Taliban established a council of ministers to administer civil matters, and Baradar held a variety of minor appointments, including deputy minister of defense and deputy head of army staff. Following the U.S. invasion of Afghanistan in October 2001, Baradar led the Taliban resistance in northern Afghanistan. He was seized in November by the Northern Alliance, a group of Afghan forces hostile to the Taliban, but freed after a short time. He later joined other top members of the Taliban, who had fled to the region near Quetta, Pakistan.

After the Taliban administration collapsed to the US-led invasion in 2001, he rose to oversee the organization's Quetta Shura in Pakistan, becoming the de facto leader of the Taliban. He was imprisoned by Pakistan in 2010, presumably because he had been considering a peace accord with the Afghan government privately, without the assistance of Pakistan. He was freed in 2018 at the request of the United States and was later designated a deputy commander of the Taliban and head of their political office in Qatar. On 15 September 2021, Baradar was recognized in Time magazine as one of the "100 Most Influential People In 2021"

Chapter 2: Volatile Region

Afghanistan, a 250,000 square miles of extremely inhospitable territory wedged between Iran and Pakistan, has been governed by the extremist Islamic Taliban organization since 1996. Negotiating, even reasoning with the Taliban has puzzled governments and international organizations ever since the group gained control following a lengthy civil war.
Only three nations; Pakistan, Saudi Arabia, and the United Arab Emirates recognized the Taliban as the legitimate government in Kabul back then during their initial tenure.

The rise of the Taliban in the mid-1990s was originally praised by many Afghans, who welcomed the group's pledge to unify the nation and stop more than 15 years of bloodshed. But strong warlords in the north, especially the Tajik leader Ahmed Shah Massoud maintained their guerilla attacks. Many Afghans have turned against the Taliban because of its oppressive brand of Islam and the violence of its leaders.

Foreign governments, alarmed by the proliferation of Islamic terrorist groups operating in Afghanistan, a rise in opium cultivation and trafficking, and disdain for human rights, shunned and isolated the country.

Pakistan

Pakistan serves as the Afghan regime's major route to the globe. Nevertheless, Pakistan seems to have very little impact on the Taliban, whose commanders are fiercely resistant to advise and pressure from outside.

Pakistan, which is controlled by an army commander who took power in October 1999, is striving to garner foreign backing to shore up its economy and portray a moderate image despite its support for the Taliban and armed insurgents battling Indian troops in the disputed border region of Kashmir. However, if the United States were to undertake an air strike or commando operation on Afghanistan to kill or capture bin

Laden, Pakistan would certainly oppose such an action publicly and not explicitly allow its territory to be used as a launching pad.

In August 1998, the United States struck numerous desert camps in Afghanistan in response to bin Laden's claimed ties to the bombings of two American embassies in East Africa. Several Pakistanis were killed and wounded in the attacks; most were reportedly being trained there for armed religious combat, possibly with funding from bin Laden.

The two countries share a long and porous border, which has served for years as a relief valve for hundreds of thousands of Afghan refugees fleeing war and drought. Pakistan is also a Muslim state; a loud and powerful minority of Muslims in Pakistan supports the Taliban, including armed extremist organizations.

Strategic connections between the two nations strengthened throughout the 1980s when Soviet soldiers seized Afghanistan and Pakistan provided as a haven for U.S.-backed opposition militants, which included Bin Laden.

India

India has no formal relations with the Taliban administration and sees it as a dangerous source of Islamic terrorism. Islamic fanatics seized an Indian airplane in 1999 and forced it to land in the Afghan city of Kandahar. Taliban authorities acted as a go-between to secure the release of most hostages in exchange for allowing the hijackers to escape. Indians attacked the government for bowing to terrorists, and since then, India has been even more hostile to the Taliban.

Saudi Arabia

If there is an epicenter of Islamic anger against the United States, it lies 60 miles south of Riyadh, Saudi Arabia, at a desert airfield where dozens of American fighter and reconnaissance planes are stationed to police southern Iraq.

U.S. planes landed in Saudi Arabia in 1990, after Iraq attacked Kuwait. They helped fight that invasion and stayed at the request of the Saudi royal family to help assure security in the Arab oil nations of the Persian Gulf despite vows to Islamic conservatives that they would return home as soon as the Iraq crisis ended.

Still nervous about Iraqi President Saddam Hussein and wary of the future of the Shiite Muslim government in nearby Iran, the Sunni Muslim-run Arab countries of the Gulf Cooperation Council have in the past decade bought tens of billions of dollars in weapons from the United States and accepted what has evolved into a permanent force of American ships, planes, tanks, and personnel.

To bin Laden and other fanatics who trained with him to battle the Soviet army in Afghanistan, the U.S. presence amounts to a contemporary crusade, an army of unbelievers in the hallowed cradle of Islam interested solely in oil resources and protecting Israel. It was the foundation of his demand for holy war against the United States, commencing after the Gulf War.

Iran

Iran maintains a crucial location between the Middle East and Central and South Asia, having a 580-mile border with Afghanistan. But it has terrible ties with the Taliban regime as well as with the United States.

Some of the biggest disagreements between Iran and Afghanistan are ideological and philosophical. Iran's hardline religious authorities rely their legitimacy on their Shiite strain of Islam, while the similarly strict Taliban officials put theirs on the dominant Sunni strain. The two nations also have severe border conflicts. Iran unhappily plays home to roughly 1.4 million Afghan refugees, mainly gathered in camps along the borders, and it is conducting a harsh battle to close its border to opium supplies from Afghanistan. Iran nearly went to war with Afghanistan in 1998, when Taliban troops assassinated 10 Iranian diplomats and an Iranian journalist in the northern Afghanistan town of Mazar-e Sharif. Some commentators have suggested that the United States should work more actively to mend ties with Iran because it may play a role in constraining unfriendly governments in Afghanistan and Iraq, other of its neighbors.

The Islamic Republic of Iran is one of the few countries in the world that refuses to establish government-to-government ties with the United States, citing numerous historical grievances, particularly the CIA's role in a 1953 coup that overthrew an elected government and installed Shah Mohammad Reza Pahlavi as ruler. The shah was ousted in the 1979 Islamic revolution, during which extremist students seized the U.S. Embassy and kept 52 U.S. Americans captive for 444 days. Relations between the two countries have never recovered.

Russia

Russia knows what it is like to go to war in Afghanistan and lose. The Soviet Union which then comprised Tajikistan, Uzbekistan, and Turkmenistan invaded Afghanistan in 1979. Years of conflict ensued until the Soviet army departed in 1989.

The struggle against the Soviets marked the beginning of the two-decade career of Bin Laden, who arrived in Afghanistan to face the Soviets with other Islamic fighters, dubbed mujahedin, and is now the reputed commander of a terrorist group claiming asylum with the Taliban.

Russia has emerged as a key opponent of the Taliban, helping to fund the protracted Afghan civil war by giving guns to opponents in the north of the nation and supporting coordinated action by other European countries against the government. Russia fears a fresh wave of unrest in the already unstable area in the aftermath of the terrorist strikes in the United States. Russian authorities claim they are already at war with Bin Laden and the troops they describe as his proxies in Chechnya, a largely Muslim territory in southern Russia that is fighting for independence. They allege Chechen insurgents have been sponsored by bin Laden and other Islamic radicals, albeit without giving clear proof.

Central Asia

The Central Asian republics that constituted the underbelly of the Soviet Union have emerged as the battlefield for an Islamic insurgency sponsored by Afghanistan that threatens to destabilize the region. In the last two years, the Islamic Movement of Uzbekistan has undertaken raids in an attempt to overturn the area's young, quasi-democratic governments and build a territory based on Islamic rule in the Ferghana Valley that spans portions of Uzbekistan, Tajikistan, and Kyrgyzstan.

The region's leaders have reacted by reinforcing their forces, sealing their borders, clamping down on internal rights, and turning increasingly to Moscow for support. The situation has led to increased tension in the strategically located region where Russia, China, and the United States are all vying for influence by coming to their aid against a common enemy.

Washington fears that the Islamic Movement of Uzbekistan powered by the Afghan drug trade, trained by the Taliban, and operating out of Tajikistan represents an arm of Bin Laden's organization and has supplied training, equipment, and political support to the governments fighting it. Russia has even stationed troops in Tajikistan.

China
China had developed increasingly close ties with the Taliban and, according to news reports, signed a memorandum of understanding for more economic and technical cooperation. The

memorandum was the most substantial part of a series of Chinese contacts with Afghanistan for years. China then had the closest contact with the isolated Kabul leadership of any non-Muslim nation, a senior Western official claimed.

China had helped create the Shanghai Cooperation Organization, which connects it with Russia and four Central Asian nations in a loose organization. One of its key missions is to fight cross-border terrorism, notably from Afghanistan. But at the same time, China has negotiated with the Taliban as part of an attempt to convince its authorities to dismantle Afghan-based facilities that are used to educate Muslim separatists from China's restive Xinjiang province. Those separatists on occasion re-enter China and conduct assaults on China's security services or civilian targets.

As part of a sweetener to obtain cooperation from the Taliban leadership, Asian officials believe, that China has dangled the promise of supplying Afghanistan with badly needed infrastructural and economic development aid. The new deal was reported. A Chinese team inked the pact in Kabul with the Taliban's mines then minister, Mulla Muhammad Ishaq.

Chapter 3:Afghanistan Civil War

Mujahideen-Taliban Era (1992–2001)

Najibullah was eventually expelled from power in April 1992, shortly after the dissolution of the Soviet Union (which had continued to give military and economic backing to the Kabul administration) (which had continued to provide military and economic assistance to the Kabul government). A coalition made mostly of the mujahideen groups that had battled the communists established a weak temporary administration, but overall peace and stability remained a distant goal. As different militias vied for control, interethnic tensions increased, and the economy lay in ruins.

Under an agreement to permit the rotation of the executive office between various groups, the presidency transferred after two months from temporary president Sebghatullah Mujaddedi to Burhanuddin Rabbani. Rabbani, however, refused to cede power to his successor following the conclusion of his two-year tenure in office. Over the following three years, rocket assaults by opposition forces, primarily those of Gulbuddin Hekmatyar, the head of the Islamic Party caused catastrophic damage to vast areas of the city. Delivery of food from foreign humanitarian agencies and the UN became critical.

The Taliban originated in the wake of the Afghan War (1978–92). Afghanistan's new government failed to create civil order outside of Kabul, and most of the nation was subject to constant extortion and attack by local militias and warlords. Facing huge relocation throughout the conflict, many Afghans found kinship in the religious discourse of the mujahideen struggle and opportunity in institutions of Islamic sciences (called madrasahs) in southern Afghanistan and northern Pakistan. In 1994 a group of former combatants, linked with a madrasah in a hamlet of Kandahār province, effectively subjugated a local warlord and started pacifying adjacent districts. The party, which had public support with its promise of security and its religious passion, gradually expanded into the movement today known as the Taliban. By late 1996 the Taliban had captured the capital, Kabul, and secured effective authority over roughly two-thirds of the nation.

The Taliban met substantial opposition, particularly once it proclaimed its interpretation of law and order. It merged a rigorous theological ideology, a combination of Deobandi traditionalism and Wahhābī puritanism, with a rigid Pashtun social code (Pashtunwali) to produce a brutally authoritarian administration. Its policies included the near-total exclusion of women from public life (including employment and education), the systematic destruction of non-Islamic artistic relics (as occurred in the town of Bamiyan), and the implementation of harsh criminal punishments. Resistance was especially apparent among non-Pashtun ethnic groups namely, the Tajik, the Uzbek, and the Hazara in the north, west, and central sections of the nation, who perceived the dominance of the mostly Pashtun Taliban as a continuation of the ancient Pashtun control of the country. By 2001 the Taliban controlled all but a tiny part of northern Afghanistan.

Rise to power(First Regime)

It is thought that the mostly Pashtun movement was originally formed at religious institutions primarily sponsored by money from Saudi Arabia, which promoted a harsh brand of Sunni Islam. Partly in reaction to this circumstance, the Taliban (Persian: "Students") arose in the autumn of 1994. The movement's spiritual and political head was a former mujahideen warrior, Mullah Mohammad Omar, who was most known for his demonstrations of devotion and involvement in the battle against the Soviet occupation. Drawing its recruits from madrasah (religious school) students in Pakistan and the southern province of Kandahār, the Taliban gained international attention when it was able to defeat those groups preying on the transit trade and when it succeeded in ridding Kandahār of its predatory and corrupt governors. The Taliban's eventual success in extending its territorial control is largely attributable to the war-weariness of the Afghan people. In a short time, others joined the students, including fighters formerly associated with the communists and several mujahideen defectors, many of whom were induced to switch sides by generous payments funded by the government of Saudi Arabia, then a major Taliban supporter.

From south-western Afghanistan, the Taliban quickly extended their influence. In September 1995, they captured the province of Herat, bordering Iran.

Exactly one year later, they captured the Afghan capital, Kabul, overthrowing the regime of President Burhanuddin Rabbani, one of the founding fathers of the Afghan mujahideen that resisted the Soviet occupation. By 1998, the

Taliban were in control of roughly 90% of Afghanistan.

Afghans, sick of the mujahideen's excesses and infighting after the Soviets were forced out, mainly welcomed the Taliban when they initially arrived on the scene. Their early popularity was largely due to their success in stamping out corruption, curbing lawlessness, and making the roads and the areas under their control safe for commerce to flourish.

The Taliban also acquired the early assistance of top Pakistani officialsincluding members of Pakistan's ISI who, together with corporations engaged in cross-border trafficking, were desperate to establish a road route through Afghanistan to markets in Central Asia. These same authorities anticipated that the installation of lucrative gas and oil pipelines from Central Asian reserves to a Pakistani endpoint would also be accomplished sooner were the Taliban to take complete control of the nation from other forces. Importantly, Taliban dominance offered

Pakistan a pliant, sympathetic administration in Kabul, which contrasted with past Afghan regimes that typically deflected Pakistani involvement in Afghanistan's internal affairs via political overtures to India, Pakistan's archrival. Despite the Taliban's mostly Pashtun membership, the absence from their agenda of the familiar irredentist Pashtun claims against Pashtun regions of Pakistan, the Pashtunistan issue made the Taliban a seemingly safe choice.

However, the Taliban's early appeal rested mainly on unifying those Pashtuns intensely angry with the Rabbani regime, which was controlled by ethnic Tajiks. Not until the Taliban ventured into areas of the country populated largely by non-Pashtuns could its wider popular acceptance be tested. Minority-dominated Herāt, Afghanistan's third largest city, fell to Taliban fighters in September 1995, and a year later the Taliban captured multiethnic Kabul, setting to flight both anti-government troops and those of Rabbani. The northern city of Mazār-e Sharīf, populated by many ethnic Uzbeks, fell in August

1998. By 2001 the Taliban's rule spread over more than nine-tenths of the nation, and in most regions under its control the militia succeeded in disarming the local populace. A fragmented alliance of mujahideen fighters known as the Northern Alliance retained control of a small area of northern Afghanistan. Fighters for the Northern Alliance, notably those under the direction of Ahmad Shah Massoud, were the sole significant hurdle to a decisive Taliban triumph.

Pakistan, Saudi Arabia, and the United Arab Emirates gave formal recognition to the Taliban government after the fall of Kabul, but the movement was denied Afghanistan's seat at the UN and came under vigorous international criticism for its extreme views, with regard to women in particular and its human rights record. The Taliban was also accused of harboring and training militants many of whom were holdovers from the war against the Soviets planning insurgencies in the Central Asian republics and China. Iran complained about the treatment of the Shī'ite Muslim people and the Taliban's suspected affiliation with gangs who transported drugs over the Iranian boundary. Pakistani authorities, although concerned about the possible ramifications of Islamic radicalism on their society, continued to assist the Taliban economically and were given varying degrees of credit for aiding the Taliban in its military successes.

Fighting between the Taliban and the Northern Alliance persisted, and the international community made little success in inducing the combatants to follow a cease-fire or in convincing the Taliban to share power in a widely represented national government. Though foreign humanitarian assistance to the Afghans continued, large-scale reconstruction was not addressed. Just as the commitment of Western organizations and donors was dubious, the competence of Taliban commanders to supervise a reconstruction effort remained doubtful. The transition from a heavily criminalized domestic and regional economy, based on smuggling weapons and narcotics and the uncontrolled exploitation of Afghanistan's natural resources remained indispensable for the country's rehabilitation and a wave of sustainable peace.

Also, the Taliban introduced or supported punishments in line with their strict interpretation of Sharia law such as public executions of convicted murderers and adulterers, as well as amputations for those found guilty of theft. Men were compelled to grow beards and women had to wear the all-covering burka.

The Taliban also outlawed television, music, and film, and disapproved of females aged 10 and above attending school. They were accused of many human rights and cultural offenses. One prominent incident occurred in 2001, when the Taliban carried on with the destruction of the famed Bamiyan Buddha sculptures in central Afghanistan, despite worldwide protest.

Pakistan has frequently maintained that it was the architect of the Taliban business, but there is no doubt that many Afghans who first joined the organization were educated in madrassas (religious institutions) in Pakistan.

Pakistan was also one of just three nations, together with Saudi Arabia and the United Arab Emirates (UAE), who accepted the Taliban while they were in power the first time round in Afghanistan. It was also the latest nation to terminate diplomatic relations with the organization. At one time, a Pakistani branch of the Taliban threatened to disrupt Pakistan from regions it controlled in the northwest. One of the most high-profile and internationally condemned of all Pakistani Taliban attacks took place in October 2012, when schoolgirl Malala Yousafzai was shot on her way home in the town of Mingora. A major military offensive two years later following the Peshawar school massacre greatly reduced the group's influence in Pakistan, though. At least three important officials of the Pakistani Taliban have been murdered in US drone operations, including the group's commander, Hakimullah Mehsud in 2013.

Chapter 4: The Beginning of a New Start

Al-Qaeda 'sanctuary'

Apart from the Taliban's unnerving disrespect for human rights, many nations were worried about the Taliban offering asylum to Osama bin Laden, who had helped create a network of foreign-born Muslim warriors during the Afghan War. That network, al-Qaeda, had grown into a network of Islamist militants who intended a violent war to liberate the Islamic world from non-Muslim influence and had staged multiple assaults against the United States. Even after bin Laden and al-Qaeda were declared guilty for the attacks on the World Trade Center in New York City and on the Pentagon outside Washington, D.C., that had happened on September 11, 2001, the Taliban refused to extradite Bin Laden.

Conditions continued to worsen in late 2001. Blame for the terrorist attacks on the World

Trade Center in New York City and a simultaneous assault on the Pentagon outside Washington, D.C., on September 11 immediately focussed on members of a Muslim extremist organization, al-Qaeda, located in Afghanistan and led by bin Laden. The Taliban rebuffed repeated U.S. efforts to repatriate bin Laden and his accomplices and demolish terrorist training centers in Afghanistan. Within weeks of the assaults, the United States and Britain initiated an extensive bombing campaign against the Taliban and gave major logistical assistance to Northern Alliance troops in an effort to compel the government to capitulate to its demands.

The Fall of the Taliban

The United States and its allies started attacking Afghanistan on the 7th of October and backed the efforts of the Northern Alliance, a group of anti-Taliban forces in Afghanistan that had been battling the Taliban's takeover of the country. In early December the Northern Alliance succeeded in ousting the Taliban administration.

Devastated by the U.S. bombardment, Taliban forces folded within days of a well-coordinated ground offensive launched in mid-November by Northern Alliance troops and U.S. special forces. On December 7 the Taliban surrendered Kandahār, the militia's base of power and the last city under its control. At nearly the same time, representatives of several anti-Taliban groups met in Bonn, Germany, and, with the help of the international community, named an interim administration, which was installed two weeks later. This administration maintained power until June 2002 when a Loya Jirga was formed that picked a transitional government to lead the country until national elections could be conducted and a new constitution established.

Many top Taliban commanders allegedly sought sanctuary in the Pakistani city of Quetta, from whence they commanded the Taliban. But the existence of what was nicknamed the "Quetta Shura" was disputed by Islamabad.

In December 2003 another Loya Jirga was assembled to review a draft constitution that had been issued in November. In January 2004, following three weeks of deliberation, the Loya Jirga passed the constitution, which provided for a directly elected president and a two-chamber legislature. It was then signed into law by Hamid Karzai, head of the transitional administration. Democratic elections, in which women were allowed the right to vote, were conducted in October 2004, and Karzai was elected president, receiving 55 percent of the vote.

In March 2005 Karzai stated that parliamentary elections will be conducted later that year. Although al-Qaeda and Taliban groups had vowed to disrupt the polls, the election took place on September 18, 2005, the first time in more than 30 years that such elections were held and in December the newly elected National Assembly started its first session. Ongoing violence throughout 2005 intensified rapidly at the year's conclusion and deteriorated substantially the following year as instability and fighting expanded.

Karzai's tenure as president was slated to end in May 2009, and at that time he was legally compelled to stand aside. Because of logistical and security reasons, however, the approaching presidential election, in which Karzai would be a candidate was postponed from May to August of that year. Karzai argued that for reasons of security he should stay in the government until the poll went held. Critics were concerned that maintaining his position would give Karzai an undue electoral advantage, and they urged him to step down as mandated by the constitution and turn power over to a temporary government. In March 2009 the Supreme Court determined that Karzai may constitutionally keep his post until the election in August. Discontent with Karzai's leadership spawned a number of presidential aspirants, however, Karzai was expertly able to neutralize or win the endorsement of most of those who may have opposed him.

The presidential election was conducted on August 20, 2009, and was followed by weeks of political instability. In September a preliminary count gave Karzai over 55 percent of the vote, therefore suggesting that he had secured an outright win over his closest competitor, former foreign minister Abdullah Abdullah. With more than 2,000 reports of fraud and intimidation, however, the United Nations-backed Electoral Complaints Commission (ECC) ordered an assessment of questionable polling stations, including those that showed a turnout over 100 percent, and opened an inquiry into fraud charges. In mid-October, the ECC concluded that the fraudulent behavior was extensive enough to invalidate votes from more than 200 polling locations. As a consequence of the verdict, roughly one-third of Karzai's votes were invalidated, and his share of the vote slid to 49.7 percent, barely below the majority he had claimed and low enough to require a second round of elections. Although Karzai originally rejected the need for a runoff, on October 20 he committed to the second round of voting between himself and Abdullah, which was planned for November 7. Shortly later, however, Abdullah withdrew from the campaign, a move he justified as being in the country's best interest. The runoff election was annulled, and soon later Karzai was inaugurated as president for a second term.

Although removed from power and split, the Taliban persisted, and many of its key members remained at large during the Afghanistan War (2001–14). (2001–14). In 2005 the Taliban started experiencing a revival, displaying hints of better coordination and durability among its members. Its founder and leader, Mullah Mohammad Omar, remained in hiding with sporadic communication, but top commanders like Mullah Dadullah and Mullah Abdul Ghani Baradar were rapidly centralizing the group's command structure. It embraced new methods patterned on those being employed by militants in the Iraq War, including the use of suicide bombers and improvised explosive devices. Recruitment was prolific, drawing on thousands of Afghans disenchanted by widespread corruption in the new Afghan government and resentment toward the casualties and destruction that accompanied the ongoing U.S. and NATO military operations.

NATO troop surge and continued stalemate

Attacks and violent confrontations between the U.S.-led coalition and the Taliban forces grew increasingly regular, notably in the eastern and southern provinces, and deaths climbed. In July 2006, North Atlantic Treaty Organization (NATO) troops replaced the U.S.-led coalition at the head of military operations in the south, and in October they also took command of the eastern provinces, thus assuming control of international military operations across the entire country. Fighting between NATO and Taliban troops persisted, and civilian deaths were widespread; in 2008 they reached their highest levels since the start of the conflict.

Insurgent attacks increased in 2009. By the middle of the year, U.S. commanders had become convinced that troop levels in Afghanistan were too low to implement their counterinsurgency strategy, which called for international forces to focus on protecting the population and securing areas for reconstruction projects, rather than simply killing large numbers of insurgents. After some debate within the Obama administration, Obama announced in December 2009 that the U.S. would temporarily increase the number of troops in Afghanistan by 30,000. This increase in troop strength would be tied to an accelerated timetable for the training of Afghan security forces and the transfer of security responsibilities from NATO to the Afghan government.

The number of NATO troops in Afghanistan peaked in 2010 at nearly 150,000. The increase in troops delivered mixed results; although NATO troops were able to sweep the Taliban out of areas that it had previously controlled, militants continued to launch devastating surprise attacks against military, government, and civilian targets. Two factors that allowed the Taliban to remain resilient despite NATO's territorial gains were the widespread unpopularity of the Afghan central government and NATO among Afghans and the presence of a safe haven for Taliban fighters across the eastern border in Pakistan.

With a military resolution to the conflict seeming increasingly unlikely and public support for the war declining in both Europe and the U.S., NATO members agreed in November 2010 to withdraw combat troops by 2014. The apparent stalemate between international troops and the Taliban also made U.S. and NATO leaders more willing to explore prospects for a negotiated political settlement with the Taliban. However, diplomatic contact between the U.S. and the Taliban in 2011 and 2012 was intermittent and failed to make progress toward an agreement. The gradual transfer of security responsibilities to Afghan forces began in 2011 and was accompanied by a significant reduction in the number of NATO troops.

Meanwhile, the situation of the Afghan central government remained precarious. Afghans' confidence in governing institutions was low, in large part because of rampant corruption at the local, provincial, and national levels. Parliamentary elections in 2010 were marred by low turnout in areas where Taliban threats kept voters away from the polls, while last-minute changes to electoral law and new allegations of vote rigging further damaged the credibility of the electoral process.

The Ashraf Ghani presidency, NATO withdrawal, and pursuit of peace

In 2014 Afghanistan held a presidential election to pick a successor to Karzai, who was constitutionally barred from seeking another term in office. As was widely expected, the start of the presidential campaign in February was met with an upsurge of insurgent violence, but the first round of voting was held on schedule in April. A runoff between the two leading candidates, Abdullah Abdullah and Ashraf Ghani followed in June. A preliminary count placed Ghani ahead, but Abdullah demanded a recount, charging that as many as two million of the ballots for Ghani were fraudulent. With both candidates claiming victory, a period of deadlock followed. In July, under pressure from the United States, both sides agreed in principle to accept the results of an internationally supervised audit of the vote and to form a national unity government in which the winner would take the position of president and the losing side would nominate someone to occupy a newly created office with powers similar to those of a prime minister. The situation, however, remained delicate; disagreements between the two sides threatened to derail the process before a final agreement could be reached.

On September 21 Ghani and Abdullah signed an agreement under which Ghani would become president and Abdullah or a nominee from his party would take the new, prime minister-like position of chief executive officer. Abdullah ultimately took the post. The position had more of an advisory role; constitutionally, its authority derived from the power of the president to delegate some presidential duties to other government members. The Loya Jirga would have to amend the constitution to formalize the post or grant it powers independent of the president.

Ghani's presidency faced a new set of issues. The end of NATO's combat mission was in December 2014, only months into his presidency. U.S. troops remained, however, to focus on training Afghan forces and assisting in counterterrorism operations. At the same time, a resurgent Taliban continued to create a challenge for the central government in maintaining authority across Afghanistan. In an attempt to stabilize the nation, Ghani's government started pursuing peace discussions with the Taliban and other armed organizations in 2015. The first official meeting between the central government and the Taliban was conducted in July. In 2016 Hizb-i Islami, the biggest militant organization after the Taliban decided to adopt the country's constitution and renounce violence in a peace accord with the central government. Many observers believed the pact might open the path for an agreement with the Taliban in the future.

In 2017 the United States raised its force deployment from 8,400 to 14,000 at the request of its top commander in Afghanistan, bolstering assistance to the central government against the Taliban and other militants. The surge failed to block the progress of the Taliban, however.

As the 2018 parliamentary elections neared, the Taliban worked to undermine the validity of the polls. They called for Afghans to boycott the elections and threatened violence at the polls. Two days before the polls slated for October 20, the Taliban assassinated the police head of

Kandahār. The polls in Kandahār were postponed by a week, while the remainder of the nation conducted elections on schedule, despite assaults on voting centers and Afghans traveling to them. In the weeks that followed, the country's electoral body revealed the results cautiously. On December 6 an electoral complaints committee ruled ballots in Kabul to be illegal, claiming fraud and incompetence, but the election commission rejected the invalidation. With about one-fourth of all votes nationwide cast in Kabul, the dispute over the city's vote endangered the legitimacy of the poll altogether. Nonetheless, despite the many challenges to the election and its outcome, a good case remained for its legitimacy: turnout was high at an estimated 4 million voters (out of 8.8 million registered), and preliminary results for the elections in Kabul were released in mid-January. Still, the election commission was dismissed for its handling of the elections, and its members were replaced by commissioners selected by the upcoming presidential election candidates. The final election results were released in May 2019.

Because of the many problems that had plagued the parliamentary elections as well as the renewed attempt toward peace talks with the Taliban, the presidential election originally set for April was pushed back twice. The election was ultimately conducted on September 28, however, despite threats from the Taliban and a lack of faith in the electoral process, participation was much lower than in previous presidential elections. Shortly after the election, main candidates Ghani and Abdullah both stated that they had earned the majority of votes. The official vote total issued in early 2020 indicated that Ghani had earned more than 50 percent of the vote, while Abdullah had received fewer than 40 percent, which Abdullah first rejected until accepting a new power-sharing pact in May.

Days after the results of the election were released, the United States and the Taliban announced that they had reached an agreement: the United States would withdraw its troops over 14 months on the condition that the Taliban would pursue peace negotiations with the Afghan government and prevent al-Qaeda and the Islamic State in Iraq and the Levant (ISIL; also called Islamic State in Iraq and Syria [ISIS]) from operating within Afghanistan. The settlement was struck on February 29, 2020, following a weeklong decrease of hostilities from both sides. In August the Afghan government agreed to a prisoner exchange with the Taliban, satisfying a fundamental criterion, pledged in February's U.S.-Taliban pact, for peace negotiations between the government and the Taliban to begin.

Negotiations between the Taliban and the central government achieved little headway, however, even when the United States commenced the departure of its soldiers in May 2021 after many months' delay. As an emboldened Taliban made significant advances despite the pullout, lack of coordination among the government's military forces and their lack of reaction to the insurgency gave the central government a crushing blow. By mid-August, the Taliban controlled practically all of Afghanistan, including Kabul.

Chapter 5: Taliban Resurgence

The Foe Within

In July 2015 the Afghan authorities found that Omar had died in 2013 in a hospital in Pakistan. Omar, who was the president of Afghanistan under the Taliban's reign and a significant Bin Ladin supporter, was sought by the US Government via the Rewards for Justice program.

His subordinate Mullah Akhtar Mansour temporarily functioned as his successor early August 2015 until he was killed in a U.S. air strike in Pakistan in May 2016. Mansur is only the second leader that the group has ever had. Hibatullah Akhundzada gained command later that month; like his predecessors, he stayed somewhat reclusive and seemed to have a minor part in organizing military activities. The violent arm of the Taliban became more controlled by the Haqqani network, whose chief, Sirajuddin, functioned as deputy leader of the Taliban.

Meanwhile, the Taliban's persistent persistence and the inability of Afghanistan's central government to exercise authority across the nation encouraged the central government to seek reconciliation with the Taliban. Officials under President. Hamid Karzai had met informally with Taliban commanders, most notably Baradar, and the first official meeting was placed under President Ashraf Ghani. The Taliban continued to regard the central government as essentially illegitimate, however and insisted on discussions with the foreign entity that had placed it: the United States.

The Afghan Taliban are responsible for most insurgent assaults in Afghanistan, which follow an established pattern of frequent low-level ambush and hit-and-run operations, paired with sporadic high-profile strikes. The Taliban have been advancing aggressively in various sections of the nation, indicated by the fact that suicide and sophisticated assaults surged by 78 percent countrywide in the first six months of 2015 compared with the same time in 2014. The Taliban between 7 and 10 August 2015 executed a series of strikes in rapid succession in Kabul that resulted in at least 60 fatalities, marking the bloodiest period in the city since the US-led invasion in 2001. In the first strike, a suicide bomber exploded a big truck bomb in a residential neighborhood while trying to target an Afghan Defense Ministry facility, killing 15 civilians and wounding up to 400 more. On its own, the explosion caused an unparalleled number of deaths from a single strike in the capital in recent years—the Taliban is generally suspected of having perpetrated the attack but they did not take credit for it because of the enormous civilian losses. Less than 24 hours later, nearly 40 cadets and bystanders were murdered when a suicide bomber disguised in a police uniform blew himself up at the entrance of Kabul Police Academy. Later that day a Taliban group struck Resolute Support Mission base Camp Integrity, killing at least nine, including one NATO serviceman. On 10 August a Taliban suicide bomber slammed a vehicle through a checkpoint at the entrance to Kabul International Airport, killing at least 5 and wounding 15.

Chapter 6: Raising an Army from the Ashes

Withdrawal of U.S. soldiers from Afghanistan.

Meanwhile, in the middle of the election count, the drive for peace negotiations was resumed in mid-December 2018. On December 17 the United States, United Arab Emirates, Saudi Arabia, and Pakistan the only countries to have a diplomatic relationship with both parties, met with the Taliban in Abu Dhabi to discuss how to advance the peace process. Just days later the United States declared its plan to remove thousands of its soldiers from Afghanistan, a move viewed by many as showing the United States' sincerity in striking a peace accord and ending the war. Afghanistan's central government had not been notified of the decision before it was revealed, however, and Afghan officials voiced amazement at the United States' lack of collaboration with the government but highlighted that Afghan troops already handled most security operations anyhow. Talks with the Taliban, however difficult at times, continued into 2019, and U.S. military levels were maintained throughout the discussions.

The United States also worked to reconcile the Taliban and the central government. Discussions were ultimately undertaken with the central government in 2019, which led in July to an agreement on fundamental principles for future discussions, but the Taliban's representatives remained focused on first achieving a settlement with the United States. They came to an agreement in principle in September, but deliberations were halted when an assault by the Taliban killed a U.S. military man.

A contract with the United States was struck in late February 2020. In return for a complete departure of U.S. troops over a 14-month period, the Taliban committed to halt its assaults against U.S. soldiers and prevent al-Qaeda, the Islamic State in Iraq and the Levant (ISIL; sometimes called Islamic State in Iraq and Syria [ISIS]), and its affiliates from functioning in Afghanistan. The accord also included a commitment to begin discussions with the central government within 10 days, but negotiations were postponed until September because of the central government's unwillingness to carry out a prisoner exchange agreed to the Taliban by the United States. Little progress was achieved throughout the discussions, which extended until 2021. Nevertheless, in April the United States restated its resolve to complete its departure, although the timetable for pullout was pushed from May to September.

Taliban Power Seizure

In February 2020, then-President Donald Trump reached a peace accord with the Taliban that includes the removal of all foreign soldiers from Afghanistan by May 2021. The deal was preserved by President Joe Biden, who extended the deadline to Aug. 31. But the withdrawal was criticized for being rushed, disorganized, and chaotic. In the year after the US-Taliban peace pact of February 2020, which was the conclusion of a protracted term of direct discussions, the Taliban seemed to adapt their tactics from intricate strikes in cities and on military outposts to a wave of targeted killings that terrorized Afghan people. The targets; journalists, judges, peace campaigners, and women in positions of authority, showed that the Taliban had not altered their radical doctrine, just their method.

Despite grave concerns from Afghan officials over the government's vulnerability to the Taliban without international support, new US President Joe Biden announced in April 2021 that all American forces would leave the country by 11 September - two decades to the day since the felling of the World Trade Center.

Having outlasted a superpower through two decades of conflict, the Taliban started conquering enormous areas of land, before once again overthrowing a government in Kabul in the aftermath of a foreign force retreating.

The organization looked to lack the numbers and firepower to retain its victories against the bigger and better-equipped military forces of the central government, but the latter's lack of coordination and lack of reaction to the insurgency enabled the Taliban to sweep the country within months. In early August, the Taliban launched an offensive, threatening government-controlled direct attacks on various metropolitan centers, including Kandahar in the south and Herat in the west. On August 6, 2021, the Taliban conquered the capital of southern Nimruz Province, the first provincial capital to fall. After it, provincial capitals started to fall in fast succession. Within days, the Taliban conquered more than ten more cities, including Mazar-i-Sharif in the north and Jalalabad in the east, leaving Kabul the only major metropolitan region under government control. On August 15, 2021, Taliban forces seized the city, prompting Afghan President Ashraf Ghani to leave the nation and the Afghan government to collapse. Later that day, the Taliban declared they had invaded the presidential palace, seized control of the city, and were creating checkpoints to preserve security.

The pace of the Taliban's territorial conquests and the collapse of both the ANDSF startled U.S. officials and allies—as well as, apparently, the Taliban itself—despite prior intelligence estimates of the situation on the ground. By mid-August, the central authority had disintegrated and the Taliban had controlled practically all of the nation, including Kabul.

They surged over Afghanistan in under 10 days, seizing their first provincial capital on 6 August. By 15 August, they were approaching the gates of Kabul. Their fast approach led tens of thousands of people to evacuate their homes, many landing in the Afghan capital, others leaving for neighboring countries.

The Taliban retook control of Afghanistan in 2021, two decades after being expelled from power by a US-led military coalition. The hardline Islamist organization surged fast throughout the nation, conquering province after province until taking the capital Kabul on 15 August last year, when the Afghan military disintegrated.

Foreign soldiers, who had promised to depart, were surprised by the rapidity of the advance and forced to hurry their exit. Many Western-backed Afghan government officials departed, as many of their countrymen and foreigners fearing Taliban domination hurried to secure a place on planes out of the country.

Departing American soldiers abandoned millions of dollars worth of weapons, trucks, and other military equipment, which was instantly captured by the Taliban as they came to power. According to one Reuters source, the Taliban grabbed possession of more than 2,000 armored vehicles, including Humvees, and up to 40 aircraft, including helicopters and drones.

The Biden administration approved the deployment of an extra six thousand soldiers to help with the evacuation of U.S. and ally forces, as well as thousands of Afghans who cooperated with the United States and were seeking to evacuate. The rapidity of the Afghan government's fall threatens a major outflow of people from Afghanistan and has worsened an already terrible humanitarian catastrophe.

The war in Afghanistan was America's longest combat, spanning over two decades. In that period, 2,248 U.S. forces lost their life and 47,245 Afghan civilians were murdered. The death toll for members of the Afghan National Army and police is 66,000, while the number of Taliban militants and other insurgents killed throughout the conflict is 51,191. According to a study by Brown University, the U.S. government spent more than $2 trillion funding the war. Yet, the U.S. and its allies were surprised and unprepared when the Taliban conquered Kabul in only a few hours. Thousands of Afghan civilians flocked to Kabul airport to escape Taliban authority.

Within weeks, the Taliban were in control of all of Afghanistan, something they had not managed to do in their first stint in power between 1996 and 2001. The Taliban's return to rule brings an end to almost 20 years of a US-led coalition's presence in the country. Kabul was the last major city in Afghanistan to fall to a Taliban offensive that began months ago but accelerated over days.

With the Taliban seemingly eager to win legitimacy both domestically and internationally, many observers hoped to see a more pliant and conciliatory regime than the one the Taliban had run before. Early indications, however, showed little resolve for change: in September it filled its transitional government with hard-liners, reopened secondary schools only for boys, and reinstituted the brutal criminal punishments for which it had been known. The leadership, meanwhile, struggled to exert unified authority throughout the organization, which for years had been operating under a decentralized command structure. The disunity made it difficult to enforce policies universally and to hold local forces accountable, leading to stark contradictions between the Taliban's public statements and its actions on the ground.

Part 2:Taliban Return

Chapter 7: The Now Afghanistan

Taliban marks 1st year back in power, but for many Afghans, there's nothing to celebrate. One year ago, the Taliban swept into the Afghan capital Kabul, as foreign forces hastily completed their withdrawal. Speaking for the Taliban at the time, Zabihullah Mujahid made a number of guarantees for the new administration.

So has the government lived up to its promises?

'We are going to enable women to work and study.... women are going to be extremely active but within the framework of Islam.'

The previous Taliban rule, in the 1990s, severely hampered women's freedom, and since the capture of power by the Taliban last year, a number of limitations have been re-imposed on women in Afghanistan. Regulations on clothes and regulations limiting entrance to public locations without a male guardian have been enforced.

In March, schools reopened for a new academic year, however, the Taliban revoked an earlier pledge, and females are presently not authorized to attend secondary school. The Taliban has cited a shortage of female instructors and the necessity to organize the segregation of facilities. This has harmed an estimated 1.1 million kids, according to the UN, and has caused intense international condemnation.

Women's involvement in the employment force has plummeted since the Taliban takeover last summer, according to the World Bank. Female involvement in the work market has climbed from 15% to 22% in slightly over a decade, between 1998 and 2019. However, with the Taliban putting further restrictions on women's travels outside the house following their return to power, the proportion of females working in Afghanistan dropped to 15% in 2021.

An Amnesty study in July concluded that the Taliban had "decimated the rights of women and children" in Afghanistan. It emphasized the violence and torture meted out to certain women who had taken part in rallies against the additional limits placed on them. In June, the UN Security Council claimed the Afghan economy had declined by an estimated 30%-40% since the Taliban takeover in August last year.

An evaluation by the government agency that monitors US-funded rebuilding operations in Afghanistan determined that while some foreign help continues to come into the country, economic circumstances remain "dire. The suspension of most international assistance and the banning of access to Afghanistan's foreign currency reserves has had major economic ramifications for the country.

To compensate, the Taliban have moved to raise tax income, as well as ramp coal shipments to take advantage of increased world prices. A three-month budget presented in January this year indicated the Taliban had received approximately $400 million in domestic income between September and December 2021. But experts have highlighted concerns regarding the lack of openness in how these numbers were gathered.

The lack of foreign backing, security concerns, climate-related issues, and global food inflation are all contributing to a fast worsening economic position.

The War on Opium

Opium production reached historic levels within a few years following the collapse of the Taliban government: it was thought that Afghanistan generated more than nine-tenths of the world's opiates. Complicating government attempts to curb production was the reality that various elements of the populace, including the Taliban and allies of the central government, benefitted from opium cultivation. Indeed, the Taliban generated a large revenue from the sector, utilizing the earnings to support their struggle.

The Taliban's commitment to eliminate opium poppy farming parallels a program they launched with some success when they were last in power more than two decades ago. Opium is needed to create heroin, and Afghanistan has been, by far, the world's greatest supply of opium for many years. In April this year, the Taliban placed a ban on the planting of poppies. There are no precise statistics on how the clampdown has been proceeding, however, reports from certain poppy-growing districts in Helmand province in the south indicate the Taliban have been compelling farmers to destroy poppy crops. A US official assessment in July stated that while the Taliban feared losing support from farmers and others engaged in the drug trade, they "look dedicated to their drugs embargo".

"There will be no manufacture of narcotics in Afghanistan….we will reduce the production of opium to zero again," claimed the Taliban administration.

However, Dr. David Mansfield, an expert on Afghanistan's drug industry, argues that the primary opium poppy crop would have been harvested by the time the embargo was enacted.

"The second [year] crop in south-western Afghanistan is normally a minor crop... therefore its destruction... will not have had a substantial effect," adds Dr. Mansfield.

It's also worth mentioning that the manufacturing and manufacture of other narcotics, like crystal meth, has been expanding, although the Taliban have outlawed a wild plant (ephedra) used to create it.

Chapter 8: Afghanistan in Chaos

Although the battle which brought the Taliban to power is mostly done, there were still over 2,000 civilian casualties (700 fatalities and over 1,400 injuries) documented between August last year and mid-June this year, according to UN figures. However, these statistics are substantially down from past years when the war was at its height.

At least 43% of the population is surviving on less than one meal a day and 97% of Afghans are predicted to be living below the poverty line by the end of this year. Some families have resorted to selling their organs for food while others have sold their children in order to live. The future appears dismal for the great majority of Afghans.

As world leaders seek to economically isolate the Taliban, their policy approaches have wrecked the economy, decimated the banking sector, and plunged the nation into a humanitarian crisis that has left more than 24 million without enough food to eat each day. The group stated that unless this is solved, the present humanitarian catastrophe might lead to more fatalities than in 20 years of conflict.

One year after Kabul fell to the Taliban, Afghanistan is in anarchy. What little progress was accomplished in the previous two decades, in terms of democracy, personal liberties, and women's rights, has been overturned. The Taliban have proved that they have not altered much from the organization that controlled in the 1990s until they were ousted by U.S.-led troops in the aftermath of the terrorist attacks of Sept. 11, 2001.

After conquering rural regions and subsequently cities over years, the Taliban poured back into the capital, Kabul, on Aug. 15 last year as the U.S.-backed President Ashraf Ghani fled.
In one short year, the economy is now on the verge of collapse, millions are jobless and near

to poverty, secondary education has been forbidden for females, women are obliged to hide their faces in public, and anybody opposing the rule risks being tortured.

And the recent execution of Al Qaeda chief Ayman al-Zawahiri in Kabul illustrates that Afghanistan remains a safe environment for violent extremists – something the Taliban had previously sworn to never allow again.

One year on

The Taliban regime has restored a severe interpretation of Islamic law since coming to power in Afghanistan. It has banned secondary education for girls. It is the only gender-based ban on schooling in the world. According to UNICEF, 3.7 million Afghan children are out of school, 60% of whom are female. With no sign the ruling Taliban will allow them back to school, some girls and parents are trying to find ways to keep education from stalling for a generation of young women. The literacy rate among girls in Afghanistan is only 37%. About a third of all Afghan girls are married before the age of 18 and are then urged to discontinue their education.

Severe restrictions have been imposed on Afghan women since the Taliban seized control last year. Women are not allowed to leave their homes without being accompanied by a male relative and must cover their faces in public. Many women have been barred from returning to their public-sector jobs and business owners have been forced to let go of most of their female staff. This has threatened the livelihood of Afghan families, as many women are the sole breadwinners.

The future for Afghans living under the Taliban's rule remains highly uncertain. While most are relieved the war is over, millions are struggling to survive. No country has recognized the Taliban government in the year since they returned to power.

The August 2021 killing in a US drone attack of al-Qaeda's leader Ayman al-Zawahiri in Kabul will do nothing to persuade Taliban critics that the group has turned over a new leaf. Hardliners in the movement seem to have the upper hand on topics such as female employment, freedom of expression, and secondary education for females, meaning that vitally needed foreign-held funds are unlikely to be released any time soon.

Civilian casualties experience a steep decline in Afghanistan

Around 50% of the fatalities since August 2021 were ascribed to the operations of the Islamic State-Khorasan (IS-K) group, a branch of the Islamic State organization currently operating in Afghanistan. In recent months, multiple IS-K assaults have taken occurred against civilians, particularly in metropolitan areas with Shia Muslim or other minority populations.

Islamic State Khorasan Province terrorists, a local branch of the Islamic State organization in Afghanistan have threatened to continue assaults now that Taliban militants are in power.

So who are these IS militants?

IS-K - Islamic State Khorasan Province - is the regional branch of the Islamic State organization. It is the most extreme and violent of all the jihadist militant groups in Afghanistan. IS-K was founded in January 2015 during the height of IS's dominance in Iraq and Syria, before its self-declared caliphate was crushed and demolished by a US-led coalition.

It recruits both Afghan and Pakistani jihadists, notably defecting members of the Afghan Taliban who don't regard their group as harsh enough.

"Khorasan" refers to a historical region covering parts of modern-day Afghanistan and Pakistan. The group previously included Pakistan until a separate Pakistan division was created in May 2019.

How many members does IS-K have?
At its height, the gang totaled roughly 3,000 combatants. However, it has sustained substantial deaths in fights with both the US and Afghan security forces, and also with the Taliban.

What assaults have IS-K carried out?

IS-K has targeted Afghan security forces, Afghan politicians and ministries, the Taliban, religious minorities, notably Shia Muslims and Sikhs, US and Nato soldiers, and foreign institutions, including charity groups. IS-K has been blamed for some of the worst atrocities in recent years, targeting girls' schools, hospitals, and even a maternity ward, where they reportedly shot dead pregnant women and nurses Unlike the Taliban, whose focus is restricted to Afghanistan, IS-K is part of the global IS network that aspires to carry out assaults against

Western, international and humanitarian targets wherever they can reach them.

Where are IS-K based?

IS-K is headquartered in the eastern region of Nangarhar, adjacent to narcotics and people-smuggling routes in and out of Pakistan. While most of its actions have been in Nangarhar and Kabul, it has also claimed assaults in the provinces of Kunar, Jowzjan, Paktia, Kunduz, and Herat.

Is IS-K tied to the Taliban?

Peripherally yes, through a third party, the Haqqani network. According to analysts, there are significant linkages between IS-K and the Haqqani network, which in turn is tightly tied to the Taliban. The guy currently in charge of security in Kabul is Khalil Haqqani who has had a $5m (£3.6m) reward on his head.

Dr. Sajjan Gohel from the Asia Pacific Foundation has been monitoring the extremist networks in Afghanistan for years.

He believes "many big strikes between 2019 and 2021 entailed coordination between IS-K, the Taliban's Haqqani network, and other terror organizations operating in Pakistan". When the Taliban seized power in Kabul on 15 August, the organization freed significant numbers of captives from Pul-e-Charki Prison, purportedly including IS and al-Qaeda terrorists. These persons are presently at large.

Why IS-K provides a threat to the Taliban

But IS-K has serious disagreements with the Taliban, accusing them of forsaking Jihad and the battlefield in favor of a negotiated peace accord thrashed out in "posh hotels" in Doha, Qatar. IS-K considers Taliban militants "apostates", making their killing lawful under their interpretation of Islamic law.

IS extremists now constitute a serious security problem for the upcoming Taliban administration, something the Taliban leadership shares in common with Western intelligence services.

The Future of Afghanistan Women in the Face of Sharia Law

In the first press conference after assuming control, a Taliban spokesperson claimed topics such as the media and women's rights will be protected **"within the context of Islamic law",** but the group has not yet offered any specifics of what that would entail in reality.

The Taliban have been noted for their rigid interpretation of Sharia, including penalties such as public executions of convicted murderers and adulterers. In the group's first press conference since seizing control of the country on Sunday, a spokesperson claimed women would be allowed to work but offered little specifics about other laws and restrictions. Zabihullah Mujahid stated that all Afghans must live **"within the framework of Islam"**.

The terrorist organization established or supported penalties in conformity with its stringent interpretation of Islam's legal system, Sharia law, while they occupied Afghanistan between 1996 and 2001. Women had to wear the all-covering burqa, and the Taliban also disapproved of females aged 10 and above attending school.

In a press conference, Mr. Mujahid faced multiple questions from the foreign media about what women's rights may look like under Taliban rule.

"We are going to enable women to work and study inside our parameters," he stated. *"Women are going to be highly involved inside our culture."*

But he did not comment when questioned about clothing standards and what responsibilities women will be allowed to play inside the country's employment. Earlier on, the Taliban declared a general amnesty across Afghanistan and said it wanted women to join its government. Analysts say the group is running a sophisticated PR campaign in an effort to win the hearts and minds of both Afghans and the international community.

The word of the new authorities has been greeted with conflicting sentiments within Afghanistan.

"I don't trust what they're saying," a lady in Kabul who saw Mujahid talk on television stated.

"It's a hoax and we're being enticed outdoors to be punished. I refuse to study or work under their regulations," stated another.

Yet several others saw some early potential.

"If we're able to work and become educated, that's the concept of freedom for me, that's my red line. That red line has not been breached by the Taliban yet," one Afghan lady stated.

"As long as my freedom to study and work is respected, I don't mind wearing a hijab. I live in an Islamic nation and I'm happy to accept the Islamic clothing code - as long as it's not a burqa however since that's not an Islamic dress code."
another said.

Mr. Mujahid further said that the Taliban were actively trying to build a government and it will be revealed in the coming days. When questioned about the likelihood of the nation hosting al-Qaeda militants or other radicals, he stated *"Afghanistan's land is not going to be used against anyone"*

The spokesperson also sought to alleviate anxieties among Afghans, pledging an amnesty for former members of the security services and those who collaborated with foreign governments

"*All their rights within Islam*", that's the slogan the Taliban have repeated innumerable times when it comes to the lives of Afghan women and girls. In recent years, Western envoys and Afghans have sought, without much success, to establish with Taliban commanders located in Doha precisely what it implies.

I've heard allusions to women's rights in traditional Arab nations such as Saudi Arabia, or Qatar. A founder member of the Taliban once shouted out that university classrooms would have to be divided, regions partitioned, with enforced head coverings. More revealing are recent allegations from rural and urban regions that women journalists have been instructed to go home, and women in offices informed their positions will now go to males. Restrictions may vary by area.

It's long been suggested that the regulations in Kabul and other more open cities may be a little different; women will now be pushing the boundaries as a new order form.

What is Sharia?

Sharia is Islam's legal system.

It is taken from the Quran, Islam's sacred book, as well as the Sunnah and Hadith - the actions and sayings of the Prophet Muhammad(SAW) (SAW). Where a solution cannot be deduced immediately from these, religious experts may provide rulings as advice on a particular subject or question.

In Arabic, Sharia literally means "the clear, well-trodden way to water". Sharia functions as a rule for life that all Muslims should adhere to, including prayers, fasting, and alms for the destitute. It tries to assist Muslims to comprehend how they should conduct every part of their life according to God's instructions.

What does this imply in practice?

Sharia may inform every area of everyday life for a Muslim. For example, a Muslim wondering what to do if their coworkers ask them to the pub after work may seek a Sharia expert for help to ensure they operate within the legal framework of their faith. Other areas of everyday life where Muslims may look to Sharia for guidance include family law, money, and business.

How are judgments made?

Like any legal system, Sharia is complicated and its application is dependent on the competence and expertise of professionals. Islamic jurists give advice and decisions. The guidance that is regarded as a formal legal judgment is termed a fatwa.

There are five distinct schools of Islamic law. There are four Sunni schools: Hanbali, Maliki,

Shafi'i, and Hanafi, and one Shia school, Jaafari. The five schools vary in how they understand the sources from which Sharia law is formed. Interpretation of Islamic law is additionally varied according to local culture and traditions, which means Sharia may seem very different in various regions.

What are examples of severe punishments?

Islamic scholars claim Sharia is mostly a rule of ethical behavior and about worship and charity but a component of it deals with crime. Sharia law separates misdeeds into two main categories: "hadd" offenses, which are major crimes with defined punishments, and "tazir" offenses, where the penalty is left to the discretion of the court.

Hadd violations include stealing, which under the strongest interpretations of Sharia, may be penalized by amputating the offender's hand.

There are several protections and a high burden of evidence in the implementation of hadd punishments but frequently doesn't happen in reality for the Taliban.

Some nations where Islamic law is enforced implement or enforce such punishments for hadd infractions, and polls have revealed views of Muslims to heavy penalties for such acts vary greatly.

Chapter 9: Muddled Water

International Concerns

The United States has an interest in seeking to sustain the considerable political, human rights, and security advances that have been gained in Afghanistan since 2001. The Taliban's control of the nation might once again transform Afghanistan into a terrorist haven since the organization is thought to have relations with al-Qaeda. The takeover also threatens to undo progress achieved in ensuring the rights of women and girls. Moreover, increased internal instability, a major migration of migrants, and a developing humanitarian catastrophe might have regional consequences if neighboring nations react. In addition, Pakistan, India, Iran, and Russia are all expected to battle for influence in Kabul and with subnational entities.

Experts warn that the Taliban represent imminent risks to Afghans' civil and political rights established in the constitution written by the U.S.-backed government. Foreign countries have warned that, if the Taliban do not safeguard Afghans' rights, they might cease delivering help, which could lead to a catastrophic humanitarian situation. Observers also worry that the Taliban might enable terrorists to operate inside Afghanistan, compromising regional and global security.

Since reclaiming authority, the Taliban have adopted steps reminiscent of their ruthless regime in the late 1990s. They have clamped down on protestors, allegedly jailed and assaulted journalists, and reinstated its Ministry for the Promotion of Virtue and Prevention of Vice, which under prior Taliban control imposed bans on conduct considered un-Islamic. The group's acting higher education minister said women would be allowed to study at institutions in gender-segregated classrooms and wearing Islamic clothing.

The Taliban also threaten progress achieved in Afghans' standards of life since the U.S. invasion. UN authorities have warned that Afghanistan is approaching collapse, as the poverty rate grows, hunger surges, and the economy dumps. Hundreds of thousands of people might evacuate their homes, joining the millions of Afghans who are already displaced. Exacerbating the issue is a stop in assistance by several nations and international organizations, which had been the lifeblood of the economy and public health system. The nation is also in the middle of a drought and the COVID-19 epidemic.

Also, foreign observers remain worried that the Taliban support terrorist groups, notably al-Qaeda, presenting a danger to regional and worldwide security. The United States attacked Afghanistan because it refused to give up Osama bin Laden, the mastermind of the 9/11 attacks. Under the Taliban's reign, Afghanistan may become a safe haven for terrorists capable of conducting strikes against the United States and its allies, experts believe, despite Taliban claims that "Afghanistan's land would not be utilized against the security of any other country."

In its 2021 report, the UN team that monitors the Taliban claimed the organization still maintains close connections with al-Qaeda. Yet, the UN experts concluded, the Taliban have begun to "tighten [their] grip over al-Qaeda by collecting information on overseas terrorist combatants and registering and restraining them." The Taliban continue to assist al-Qaeda with security in return for resources and training. Between two hundred and five hundred al-Qaeda members are reported to be in Afghanistan, and its commanders are believed to be stationed in locations around the Afghanistan-Pakistan border. Many members of the Taliban's provisional government had collaborated with al-Qaeda; others are thought to have contacts to this day.

At the same time, the Taliban have been battling against its adversary, the Islamic State in

Khorasan, a terrorist organization with up to 2,200 militants in Afghanistan. Experts believe that the terrorist organization would continue to commit attacks on the nation even as the Taliban attempt to destroy it. Amid the U.S. military pullout, the Islamic State in Khorasan claimed responsibility for an assault near the Kabul airport that killed 13 U.S. service personnel and at least 170 Afghan civilians.

Mujahid said neither al-Qaida nor any of its members are present in the nation, stating they all fled Afghanistan for their original countries following the October 2001 U.S.-led military assault. Washington charges leaders of the terrorist network for orchestrating September 11, 2001, assaults on America from then-Taliban-ruled Afghanistan. At the time, only three nations; Pakistan, Saudi Arabia, and the United Arab Emirates had recognized the Taliban. During its tenure from 1996-2001, the organization had fully excluded women from public life and girls from acquiring an education, contributing to Afghanistan's diplomatic isolation.

Mujahid repeated Kabul's vow that it would not allow anybody to endanger the U.S. and its allies by utilizing Afghan land. "We are ready for this, but only if additional efforts are done to create confidence and improve political ties."

A United Nations assessment indicated some months ago the Taliban continued to retain tight relations with al-Qaida, pointing to the alleged presence of the network's "core leadership" in eastern Afghanistan, including its commander, Ayman al-Zawahri. The assessment concluded, however, that neither al-Qaida nor the Islamic State Khorasan Province (ISIS-K) "is assessed to be capable of undertaking foreign assaults until 2023 at the earliest, regardless of their aim or of whether the Taliban moves to constrain them."

Structure of The Taliban regime

In September 2021, the Taliban proclaimed a provisional government composed of hard-line leaders. The regime will be known as the Islamic Emirate of Afghanistan, and the Taliban previously said the government will be led by a religious leader and draw its legitimacy from clerics. They have not mentioned holding elections. (Under the U.S.-backed government, Afghanistan was an Islamic republic that was led by a president and drew legitimacy from universal suffrage in accordance with international laws and norms.) No women or officials from the preceding government and only a few representatives from ethnic minority communities were included in the Taliban's cabinet. Experts say it is unlikely that the Taliban will meaningfully share power with any former government officials.

The Now-Leader of Taliban

The Taliban's leadership council is called the Rahbari Shura and is better known as the Quetta Shura, named for the city in Pakistan where Mullah Mohammed Omar, the Taliban's first leader, and his top aides are believed to have taken refuge after the U.S. invasion. (Omar died in 2013 and was succeeded by Mullah Akhtar Mohammad Mansour, who was killed in a 2016 U.S. airstrike in Pakistan.) The council makes decisions for all "political and military affairs of the Emirate," according to the UN monitor. It is presently commanded by Mawlawi Hibatullah Akhundzada, who has not been seen publicly in years.

The leadership council controls numerous commissions, akin to the ministries in operation previous to the Taliban's fall, and administrative organs through which the Taliban manage a shadow government. The commissions concentrate on subjects like economy, education, health, and outreach. The military committee picks shadow governors and combat commanders for each of Afghanistan's thirty-four provinces. The political commission conducted peace discussions with the United States and has been situated in Doha, Qatar.

The Taliban's new thirty-three-member caretaker government comprises members who are deemed terrorists by the United States and who are sanctioned by the United Nations. Mohammad Hassan Akhund, who was close with Omar and occupied various prominent jobs over the last two decades, is interim prime minister. Taliban co-founder Mullah Abdul Ghani Baradar, who chaired the Taliban's political committee, is Akhund's deputy. Sirajuddin Haqqani—who is the acting leader of the Haqqani Network, a terrorist organization in Afghanistan's southeast and Pakistan's northwest with strong links to the Taliban, al-Qaeda, and Pakistan's intelligence services—is the acting interior minister. Mullah Muhammad Yaqoub, Omar's son, is the acting defense minister.

Do Afghans support the Taliban?

For years after they collapsed from power, the Taliban had support. The Asia Foundation, a U.S.-based nonprofit organization, reported in 2009 that half of Afghans, mostly Pashtuns and rural Afghans had sympathies for armed opposition organizations, notably the Taliban. Afghan support for the Taliban and related organizations derived in part from complaints against official institutions.

But in 2019, a response to the same poll indicated that just 13.4 percent of Afghans felt an affinity for the Taliban. As intra-Afghan peace talks stalled in early 2021, an overwhelming majority surveyed said it was important to protect women's rights, freedom of speech, and the current constitution. Around 44 percent of Afghans surveyed said they believed that Afghanistan could achieve peace in the next two years.

Following the 2021 takeover, tens of thousands of Afghans tried to escape Afghanistan, and the UN refugee agency said more than half a million Afghans could flee by the end of the year. In addition, a resistance movement of former officials, local militia members, and Afghan security forces who call themselves the National Resistance Front formed in the remote and mountainous Panjshir Province. The Taliban took control of the province after more than a week of fighting, but the resistance group has vowed to continue opposing the Taliban.

Chapter 10: Afghanistan Economy on the Brink of Collapse

Diplomatic Recognition

Afghanistan's Taliban have said the United States is impeding their road to winning international recognition for the Islamist group's new government in Kabul.

"As far as recognition by other nations is concerned, I believe the United States is the largest obstacle," leading Taliban spokesperson Zabihullah Mujahid said when asked to clarify whether his group's policies or any country was responsible for the delay in earning legitimacy.

"It [America] does not let other nations progress in this direction and has itself not made any step on this count either," he stated while replying to reporters' queries through a Taliban-run WhatsApp group for reporters.

Mujahid asserted that the Taliban had satisfied **"all the requirements"** for their administration to be accorded international recognition. He claimed all nations, including the United States, need to grasp that political engagement with the Taliban is in **"everyone's interest."** It would enable the world to officially address "the grievances" they have with the Taliban. Mujahid said Taliban leaders "want better" bilateral relations with the U.S. in keeping with the deal the two nations struck in Doha, Qatar, in February 2020. Washington also has to strive toward creating stronger connections with Kabul, he added.

"We were enemies and fighting the United States so long as it had occupied Afghanistan. That war has ended now," he said.

The Taliban have sought to boost diplomacy with countries in the region, such as China, Pakistan, and Russia. They have encouraged countries to keep their embassies open and foreign businesses to continue work in

Afghanistan. However, the United States and other Western countries have not yet recognized the Taliban as Afghanistan's government nor have they defined what kind of relationship they will have with the Taliban. U.S. Secretary of State Antony Blinken said the United States will "judge [the Taliban's cabinet] by its actions." Chinese officials have said that China's support for Afghanistan will partly depend on the Taliban preventing terrorist activities in the region.

No country has yet recognized the Taliban as legitimate rulers of the country, mainly over their harsh treatment of Afghan women and girls. The group is also being pressed to govern the country through a broad-based political system where all Afghan groups have their representation to ensure long-term national stability.

Since taking control of Afghanistan 12 months ago, the Taliban have suspended secondary education for most teenage girls and prevented female staff in certain government departments from returning to their duties.

The Ministry for Vice and Virtue, tasked with interpreting and enforcing the Taliban's version of Islam, has ordered women to wear face coverings in public. Women are barred from traveling beyond 70 kilometers unless accompanied by a male relative. The Taliban have rejected calls for removing the curbs on women and Mujahid also defended them.

"The orders… regarding women are in accordance with [Islamic] Shariah, and these are the rules of Shariah," he asserted.

The Taliban are "religiously" obliged to implement Islamic Sharia to counter practices that Islam prohibits, Mujahid said, without elaborating.

"Hopefully Afghan women will also not make demands for things that are against the principles of Islam." he said

Afghanistan's immediate neighbors and regional countries also have urged Taliban authorities to ease their restrictions on women before they could consider opening formal ties with Kabul.

"[An] inclusive ethnopolitical government should be the first step toward this. We make no secret of this, and we say so outright to our Afghan partners," Zamir Kabulov, Russian special envoy for Afghanistan, said earlier, when asked whether Moscow was close to giving the Taliban legitimacy. Additionally, scholars in many Islamic countries have disapproved of the Taliban's ban on female education and other policies limiting women's access to public life.

Taliban's money and foreign backing

Until their takeover, the Taliban largely made cash via criminal activities, including opium poppy farming, drug trafficking, extortion of local companies, and abduction, according to the

UN monitoring agency. Estimates of their yearly revenue vary from $300 million to $1.6 billion. According to one estimate, they generated roughly $460 million from opium poppy farming in 2020. They have also supplemented their revenue with clandestine mining and contributions from overseas, despite tight UN sanctions. It is unknown how the Taliban's financial streams would evolve under the new rule.

Many experts say the Pakistani security establishment continues to give financial and logistical support to the Taliban, including providing sanctuary to Taliban militants, to counter India's influence in Afghanistan. Islamabad dismisses these charges. (At the same time, Pakistan has battled its insurgency group, Tehrik-e-Taliban Pakistan, which is sometimes referred to as the Pakistani Taliban and is distinct from the Afghan group.)

Now that the Taliban have reportedly taken full control of Afghanistan and begun forming a government, a looming challenge awaits: How will they keep their country and economy afloat financially?

For the past 20 years, the U.S. government and other countries have financed the vast majority of the Afghan government's non-military budget and every cent of the fighting force that melted to the Taliban so quickly in August 2021. Now, with American aid likely out of the question and billions in central bank foreign reserves frozen, the Taliban will have to find other means to pay for salaries and support citizens and infrastructure.

According to an expert who has been examining the finances of the Taliban and American-backed administration for many years as an economic policy researcher at the Center for Afghanistan Studies. Understanding how the Taliban will pay for their administration starts with the last time they were in power over 20 years ago.

Afghanistan has changed a lot In the 1990s, Afghanistan was a vastly different nation. The population was under 20 million and depended on foreign assistance agencies for the limited services they could supply. In 1997, for example, the Taliban administration had a budget of only US$100,000, which was barely enough for the salaries of government personnel, much alone the whole country's administrative and development demands.

Today, Afghanistan has altered considerably. The population has risen dramatically, and its residents gradually grew to anticipate amenities such as health care, education, and basic utilities. In 2020, for example, Afghanistan had a non-military budget of $5.6 billion. As a consequence, Kabul has been converted from a war-ravaged metropolis into a contemporary metropolis, with an increasing number of high rises, internet cafés, restaurants, and universities.

Most of the developmental and infrastructural expenditure that has taken place since 2001 has come from other nations. The U.S. and other foreign donors financed nearly 75% of the government's non-military expenditures during those years. In addition, the U.S. invested $5.8 billion since 2001 for economic and infrastructural development. Still, government income was starting to fund a larger percentage of domestic expenditure in recent years. Sources included customs charges, taxes, money from fees on services like passports, telephones, and highways, as well as revenue from its immense but mainly undeveloped mineral resources.

Revenue would have been a lot higher were it not for the government's pervasive corruption, which some analysts and officials regard as a fundamental factor in its demise. A study from May 2021 stated that $8 million was being embezzled out of the nation every day, which would total up to nearly $3 billion a year.

Afghanistan's Difficulties

But fighting the battle may be simpler than controlling the county, which has numerous issues. Afghanistan is now facing a severe drought that threatens over 12 million people – a third of the population with "crisis" or "emergency" levels of food poverty. Prices for food and other needs have skyrocketed, while most banks have begun to reopen with limited cash availability. And like many nations, its economy has been hit by COVID-19 – and some predict a rise in cases as vaccination rates plummet. Many public health institutions confront serious budget problems.

The Taliban also confront enormous financial constraints. Roughly $9.4 billion in Afghanistan's international reserves were frozen immediately after the Taliban took over Kabul. The International Monetary Fund withheld more than $400 million in emergency reserves, while the European Union paused plans to transfer

$1.4 billion in assistance to Afghanistan until 2025.

5 probable financing sources for future Afghanistan administration

Still, while they complete forming their government and determining a future path, the Taliban have a few sources they may be able to tap to earn enough money to manage their regained country:

- **Customs and taxes.** Now that the Taliban are in complete control of Afghanistan's border crossings and government buildings, they can begin collecting all imports and other taxes.

- **Drugs.** The Taliban has declared it won't allow Afghan farmers to cultivate opium poppies as they seek worldwide legitimacy for their authority. But they may alter their mind if that acknowledgment doesn't come, in which case they may be able to continue to make a large stream of cash from drug smuggling. Afghanistan is claimed to be responsible for around 80% of the worldwide opium and heroin supply.

- **Mining.** Afghanistan is projected to contain $1 trillion worth of minerals in its mountains and other sections of the nation. China in particular has been keen to mine for these metals, which include ones that are vital to the contemporary supply chain, such as lithium, iron, copper, and cobalt. This may not be achievable in the near term, however.

- **Non-Western nations.** Several governments have been reportedly helping the Taliban financially, including Russia, Qatar, Iran, and Pakistan, and these countries may continue to do so. After the previous Afghan government collapsed in August, It was said by an ex-central bank official that a country in the region, likely Qatar, injected millions of dollars to support the Afghan economy. China in particular stands out for its possible links to the incoming regime since the Taliban have lately called the nation their "principal partner." On Sept. 8, 2021, China offered the government $31 million in emergency help. Besides extracting minerals, China is also interested in expanding its Belt and Road Initiative - a worldwide infrastructure development project – into Afghanistan.

- **Western help.** Even with these alternative sources of money, I think the Taliban will still be hungry to restore funding from the U.S. and other Western nations and get rid of United Nations sanctions that have been in place since 1999. The Taliban have declared they want to act differently than in the 1990s, particularly by respecting the rights of women and not enabling terrorists to operate from

Afghanistan. And the EU, U.S., and other nations may wish to use assistance and frozen deposits as leverage to keep the Taliban to these pledges.